STRATEGIC
PLAY

STRATEGIC PLAY

THE CREATIVE FACILITATOR'S GUIDE VOLUME #12
NOW WHAT THE DUCK?

ACTIVITIES FOR ENGAGEMENT EXTENDED
WITH THE 6 DUCK BRICKS

Jacqueline Lloyd Smith, MA, MBA, CMC, FRSA
Stephen J. Walling, CEC, FRSA

Copyright © 2023 by Jacqueline Lloyd Smith and Stephen J. Walling
Edited by Andrea Brittain
All rights reserved

LEGO® Copyright

LEGO® and LEGO® SERIOUS PLAY® are trademarks of the LEGO® Group 2017.

This book is not approved, authorised or endorsed by the LEGO Group. LEGO®, the LEGO® logo, the Brick, Knob, configuration and the Minifigure are trademarks of the LEGO® Group 2015.

LEGO® SERIOUS PLAY® trademark guidelines: *www.lego.com/en-us/seriousplay/trademark-guidelines*

This book uses and builds on the LEGO® SERIOUS PLAY®

Open Source Guide made available by the LEGO Group under a Creative Commons licence ('Attribution Share Alike' see *creativecommons.org/ licenses/by-sa/3.0/ for licence details).*

www.strategicplay.com
hello@strategicplay.com

ISBN: 978-1-78324-297-9

All rights reserved. Apart from any use permitted under UK copyright law, this publication may not be reproduced, stored or transmitted by any means, without prior permission of the copyright holder/publisher.

Whilst every effort has been made to ensure that the information contained within this book is correct at the time of going to press, the author and publisher can take no responsibility for the errors or omissions contained within.

A CIP catalogue record for this book is available from the British Library

Published by Wordzworth *www.wordzworth.com*

CONTENTS

Introduction — vi

    Activity Name: Calling All Ducks! — 1
    Activity Name: Duck, Networking — 7
    Activity Name: Mind Your Ducking Language — 9
    Activity Name: Duck LEGOcy — 12
    Activity Name: Ducking Around — 16
    Activity Name: How the Duck Are You? — 19
    Activity Name: Ducking Paradise — 22
    Activity Name: Get the Duck out of Here — 26
    Activity Name: The Karduckians — 30
    Activity Name: Where the Duck Are You? — 33
    Activity Name: Superhero Duck — 37
    Activity Name: Ducking Details — 41
    Activity Name: Ducking Values — 44
    Activity Name: I Need a Ducking Holiday — 47
    Activity Name: Duck Hunting — 50
    Activity Name: Flocking the Duck — 54
    Activity Name: Rock the Duck — 57
    Activity Name: ProDucktivity — 59
    Activity Name: Get Your Ducks in a Row — 62
    Activity Name: Management, Duck Success — 65
    Activity Name: SNADU (Situation Normal All Ducked UP) — 68
    Activity Name: Beyond the Duck Pond — 71

Joy & Happiness with Bricks — 75

    LEGO® Duck Connection — 75
    Power of Color — 77
    Deconstructing — 79
    The Sound of Bricks — 81
    Organizing Bricks — 83
    The Curious Little LEGO Duck — 86

Conclusion — 87

References — 88

INTRODUCTION

Welcome to the world of *Now What the Duck!* Since 2016, the landscape of duck activities has undergone a profound transformation, expanding its relevance within traditional workshops and training classrooms as well as in the dynamic realm of online work and diverse global cultures. As we look back, we recognize our journey has been enriched by numerous new activities and a plethora of stories from the field, which serve to underscore the universal applicability of these concepts.

It is simply ducking expansive!

Our portfolio now includes a multitude of fresh activities, each tailored to address specific learning and problem-solving objectives along with individual and team reflections. These activities have been meticulously developed, tested, and refined to ensure their effectiveness in both virtual and in-person settings. Our ever-growing toolbox is equipped to engage participants in a variety of ways, fostering creativity, collaboration, and innovation.

One particularly noteworthy addition to our repertoire is the successful implementation of these playful methodologies within the United States Air Force's training programs in different bases. We were honored to take the ducks out of the galaxy in a joint project called "Space Force: Designing Space." Working with the Department of Defense, we used design thinking to test threat scenarios for Space Force. The department's willingness to embrace our methods highlights the adaptability and efficacy of our tools, even within high-stakes, mission-critical contexts. The duck has even played with us at NASA in the Jet Propulsion Lab.

Beyond our borders, we have witnessed the seamless integration of duck activities in diverse cultural settings around the world. These cross-cultural experiences have illuminated the universal appeal of play as a catalyst for learning and growth. Our stories have ranged from the bustling streets of Tokyo and Hong

Kong to the remote regions of Africa, South and Central America, and Canada. This attests to the profound impact of play in breaking down barriers, fostering understanding, and stimulating creative thinking.

As we continue to chart new territories in the realm of playful learning, we remain committed to sharing our evolving insights and experiences. The journey of duck activities has evolved into a global adventure, marked by innovation, cultural enrichment, and a shared commitment to harnessing the power of play for personal and professional development.

If you are reading this book, we suspect you already understand the transformative potential of play. This is truly wonderful. If you are new to this method, we extend a warm welcome to the dynamic and continually evolving realm of playful learning.

Our commitment to enhancing your experience with the duck activities has led to this expanded offering of a wide array of supplementary activities, all utilizing the same modest set of materials. This ensures flexibility and adaptability to suit various learning needs and time constraints.

Our journey through the world of playful learning and duck activities has been a thrilling one. Whether you are an experienced advocate of play or a newcomer eager to embrace its transformative power, we hope this book will inspire you. This expansion of activities and the stories from the field reflect our deep commitment to fostering creativity, curiosity, and collaboration in a constantly-evolving world. As you embark on your own adventures in playful learning, remember the power of play knows no bounds. It has the remarkable ability to unlock potential, dissolve barriers, and elevate our understanding of the world. So go forth and play. For it is in play we find the seeds of innovation, growth, and endless possibilities.

A SPECIAL NOTE TO TEACHERS

For educators who have embarked on the noble journey of shaping young minds, we acknowledge the extraordinary role you play in nurturing future generations. The integration of playful learning methods, as presented in this book, can be a powerful tool in your educational arsenal.

As you delve into these pages, consider the profound impact of play on your students' engagement and comprehension. While the activities outlined here can certainly add a touch of fun to your classroom, they also hold the potential to ignite a spark of curiosity, creativity, and critical thinking that can last a lifetime.

We encourage you to explore and adapt these playful techniques to suit your unique teaching context. Be it in a traditional classroom or a virtual learning environment, the principles of playful learning can bridge gaps, break down barriers, and inspire a lifelong love of learning.

Thank you for your unwavering dedication to education and for being a guiding light in the lives of countless young learners. Your commitment to embracing new methodologies, like those presented here, ensures the joy of learning continues to flourish in classrooms around the world.

READY FOR SOME MORE DUCKING FUN?

Take six small LEGO® bricks and add some even more interesting instructions. You can provide your group with some wonderful activities. Do not be fooled into thinking you need a larger number, for it is amazing what you can do with just six bricks. We also have included expanded activities so you can bring in additional bricks and other fun materials.

Here are just a few of the activities you can do with a set of LEGO Duck Bricks.

Time to use the "duck" word!

ACTIVITY NAME: CALLING ALL DUCKS!

As published in our previous book, Strategic Play: The Creative Facilitator's Guide#2: What the Duck

Why Use

To provide immediate evidence of the power of diversity of thought and to illustrate that everyone is creative.

When to Use

Anytime you want to take people out of their comfort zones and use a new modality and function for learning and experiencing.

Resources

The LEGO® duck bricks to make a duck (for each person)

Time

Approximately 5 minutes:

.5 minute to give the instructions
1 minute to build a duck
2 minutes for the debrief
1 minute to remind people of the power of creative thinking

Group Size

1 +

Instructions

1. Give the builder(s) the six LEGO® duck bricks
2. Tell them they have one minute to build a duck.
3. When the duck is complete (or in one minute) stop the building and comment on how the duck is perfect.

Remember, if the builder says they built a duck we all consider it to be a duck. There is no right or wrong duck builder.

Debrief One

Congratulate everyone for making such great ducks.

Have people look at their ducks and compare them with the other ducks. Ask if any two ducks look exactly the same.

Of course, all ducks are going to be different given the multiple mathematical combinations of bricks.

Now make the point that to think of solutions to problems facing the world today, we need all types of thinking and all ideas. The ducks represent the different ways to solve a problem when everyone has the same resources. We need all the ideas to be successful as we try to solve more and more complex problems.

Debrief Two

Ask what happened in one minute. What did they need to do to build the duck? You will get a variety of answers, including but not limited to:

1. I had to think of what a duck looks like (information retrieval from long-term memory).
2. I needed to look at my inventory and consider how I might build a duck (symbolic representation).
3. I discovered the eye and that helped me to think.
4. I found the red parts and thought they must be wings or flippers.
5. I needed to put the bricks together (fine motor skills).
6. I needed to build and change the ideas (rapid ideation and prototyping).
7. I needed to defer judgment and try to build.
8. I needed to control my emotions (panic, fear, and excitement) to stay focused (executive functioning).

9. I had to encourage myself to keep going and relax (resiliency and the ability to encourage self to stay with a difficult task)
10. I started to look at other people's ducks (I did some informal market research).
11. I had to do something—so many times we do nothing.
12. I had to manage my time, because we only had one minute.
13. I had to manage my own expectations of perfection.
14. I had to remind myself this was a safe environment (psychological safety).
15. I wanted to be finished first. I wondered if this was a race or a contest.
16. I was not happy with my build but I kept building until the last second, working towards improvements.

All this happens in only one minute. You have demonstrated the power of play and the diversity of thought. Many organizations focus on cultural diversity but diversity of thought seems to create the most conflicts. Using this one minute duck build is an excellent way to demonstrate some simple points:

- Everyone had the same materials.
- Everyone had the same amount of time.
- Everyone had the same instructions.
- Everyone built something different.

The ducks are all very different, why? When people can answer and say it is because we think differently, you can build on the concept that this is what frequently happens in organizations and communities. We all think differently and interpret things differently. This is one of the most interesting points of human nature.

What would the world look like if we all thought alike? Would we have good ideas? Would we have different ways to solve problems? Would our thinking be narrow or broad?

How often does the leader send out a memo, which everyone then reads and interprets differently? After reading it, they take that information and feel one way or another about it and then behave accordingly, thus affecting the results. When people get the same information but interpret it differently, they make assumptions that are hard to check because they think everyone made the same assumptions. When people see others doing things they interpret as wrong they then make the assumption these wrong people are acting with the intention to cause harm. This gives us the makings of a conflict.

When you use the duck to illustrate diversity of thought you can make the point that everyone's duck is perfect. We can learn so much from people who have built ducks that are different from ours.

It is not about having the same duck. It is about having the freedom and openness to build a duck that belongs to us, that has our fingerprint, and that we can value and appreciate just like our ideas, thoughts, methods, and opinions. Having different ducks and stories does not make anyone wrong. This is about understanding that people think differently. Diversity of thought gives us the power to build a duck and build a better organization, a better community, and a better world.

Debrief Three

Ask everyone to look at the duck and give it some love, because the duck represents what our mind was thinking one minute ago. Rarely do we see our thoughts because they come and go so quickly. This process allows us to not only think, but to mull over what we were thinking about.

Online

This activity works great online . To do this well, ship people bags of multiple bricks and include the duck bricks inside the bag. Then have them find the duck bricks and run the above activity. Do not put a photo of the duck on the bag. If you do, they will just rebuild the photo.

Very Large Groups

We put this activity to the test in Calgary, Alberta at the $nventures Conference. The organizers asked us to give an opening activity for over 2,000 people who were attending the conference. The first challenge was coming into possession of 2,000 ducks. With a little help from our friends at the LEGO Systems Group in Denmark, we were able to acquire 2,000 packets. The tables were large and round, seating 8 – 10 at each. Our presentation on the Power of Play was only 30 minutes long, so we needed to distribute the ducks before we began. Because the conference organizers also asked us to run a panel discussion, we were able to invite some clients to speak. Sarah D. Moyle (Intel) and Richard Perez (Procter and Gamble) joined us and we put them to work before the doors opened.

We created multi-colored gift bags and distributed them, one per table. Each bag contained 8 – 10 duck packets. After a short presentation on the Power of Play, we asked people to distribute the ducks around their table and the fun began.

ACTIVITY NAME: CALLING ALL DUCKS! | 5

ACTIVITY NAME: DUCK, NETWORKING

Why Use

This is a fun activity to use when you want to mix people up, connect a group, add some engagement, or just have some fun. Most people do not like networking and making small talk, so this activity can make that process easier and more enjoyable.

When to Use

This is a great opener for a new group, a conference, a training, or the first day of class.

Resources

The LEGO® duck bricks to make a duck (for each person)
Timer
Bell /Chime
Microphone (optional)

Instructions

1. Give each participant a set of LEGO® duck bricks.
2. Follow the instructions from "Calling All Ducks."
3. Ask people to meet someone new and introduce their ducks and themselves. Remind them this is like speed dating: Once you meet and introduce yourselves to each other, change partners.
4. Ask them to look at the other person's duck to see if they are the same or different.

5. Challenge them to see how many authentic and meaningful connections they can make.
6. You can also ask them to collect business cards.
7. Keep the room moving by timing each new pairing for about 4 minutes; ring the bell or chime to indicate the next pair change.
8. When you feel they have made enough connections, ask everyone to return to their seats.

Note: This can be a very noisy activity. That is why we recommend using a bell/chime to indicate the change of partners. And it is also why you may want a microphone to ask people to return to their seats.

Debrief

Ask the room to answer these questions. If it is a large group, you can ask for a show of hands:

1. Ask who met someone they didn't know before.
2. Ask who met more than 2 people, 3 people, 4 people, etc.
3. Ask if they found anyone with the same duck or one that was similar.
4. Ask what role the duck played in this networking activity.
5. Ask how many business cards they collected.
6. Ask if they made a connection they would like to reconnect with.

ACTIVITY NAME: MIND YOUR DUCKING LANGUAGE

Why Use

To work with people who need help with language, including children, second language learners, or people being retrained in speech and language due to an illness or disability. To encourage language development through storytelling and expression.

When to Use

You can use this anytime you want to use fun storytelling as a way to help someone increase their ability to share stories, ideas, and use new words.

Resources

The LEGO® duck bricks to make a duck (for each person)
Paper and pen or pencils to capture ideas.

Time

Approximately 20 minutes:

1 minute to give the instructions
2 minutes to build a duck
2 minutes to modify the duck
10 minutes for story building as per the instructions below
2 minutes for sharing
3 minutes for debrief and reflection

Group Size

1+

Instructions

1. Give the builder(s) the six LEGO® duck bricks
2. Explain they have one minute to build a duck.
3. When the ducks are complete, or in one minute, stop the building and comment on how the ducks are perfect.
4. Ask them to add a decoration to the duck to make it more interesting, maybe a flower or a hat.
5. Ask them to give the duck a name, like Fred or Frederica.
6. Ask them to give the duck an action. what is the duck doing? It might be walking, dancing, or shopping.
7. If you are teaching particular words, you can ask the builders to add these words to the story to create something fun and interesting. Give them time to find additional duck parts, as needed, so they can build a more complete story.

Remember: If the builder says they built a duck, we all consider it to be a duck. There is no right or wrong duck or duck builder.

Debrief

- Congratulate everyone for making such great ducks and duck stories.
- Ask for volunteers who would like to share their story with the group.
- Invite others to ask questions about the duck.

Online

This activity works great online. To do this well, ship people bags of multiple bricks and include the duck bricks inside the bag. Then have them find the duck bricks and run the above activity. Do not put a photo of the duck on the bag. If you do, they will just rebuild the photo.

ACTIVITY NAME: DUCK LEGOCY

Why Use

This is a great improvisation and storytelling activity.

When to Use

You can use this anytime you want people to have fun together, think about their work, and have an influence.

Resources

The LEGO® duck bricks to make a duck (for each person)
Post-it Notes
Sharpies

Time

Approximately 40+ minutes:

1 minute to give the instructions
2 minutes to build a duck
5 minute to write words on a Post-it
2 minutes to change seats
2 minutes to give an example
15 minutes storytelling
10 minutes for the debrief

ACTIVITY NAME: DUCK LEGOCY | 13

Group Size

2+

Instructions

- Ask everyone to build a small duck.
- When the time is up, ask the participants to hold up their ducks to see if any are identical. Make comments about how the ducks are perfect and the diversity of thinking styles they represent.

Round One

- Ask your participants to name their ducks.
- Tell them the duck is retiring from its job at XYZ (you can get creative and theme this around the group you are with).
- Participants must silently write three descriptive words about what the duck is proudest to leave behind as they retire.

Round Two

- Once they have written their three words, ask them to stand behind their seats.
- Once everyone is standing, ask them to move one seat to the right and sit back down.
- Explain they are at the duck's retirement party and they are the duck's very good friend.

Round Three

- Read the three words on the Post-it Note and quickly make a speech to celebrate the duck's retirement. Do not just read the words. Weave them into a short story or toast.
- Clap for each storyteller as they finish and then move to the next person. Continue until everyone has shared a retirement story.

Round Four

- When the stories are done, everyone moves back to their original seat.
- Give everyone a chance to talk and laugh.

Debrief

- Ask if everyone had a chance to create and tell a story.
- Ask if everyone was able to make up a short story to share.
- Use this as an example of how quickly our brains can work while thinking with our hands, simply by looking at three words and an object.
- Use this as an example of the powerful nature of storytelling. Expand on the topic as much as you like because it fits well into many leadership or brand applications.

Note: Our dear friend Laura was the inspiration for this activity. After being exposed to LEGO® SERIOUS PLAY® methods (LSP) during a training, she exclaimed that she was changing her name to Laura 2.0. She even wrote this new name on her name tag She explained that she was seeing the world in an entirely new light after experiencing LSP. She made a short promotional video for us, where she tells us that she is now going to leave her "LEGOCY." Laura now lives and plays on the Ocean in Thailand, and we will always remember her as Laura 2.0

ACTIVITY NAME: DUCKING AROUND

Why Use

This is a fun activity to use when you want to stress the importance of using visual tools to aid the process of clear communication.

When to Use

When you want people to think about and reflect on how we all communicate and how different thinking styles cause people to make different assumptions while providing information.

ACTIVITY NAME: DUCKING AROUND | 17

Resources

The LEGO® duck bricks to make a duck (for each person)

Instructions

1. Give everyone a set of LEGO® duck bricks.
2. Divide the group into two halves: builders and nonbuilders.
3. Ask the nonbuilders to stand with their LEGO® bricks and turn their backs to those who are building so they cannot observe.
4. Ask the builders to make a duck (hidden from the others) and remind them, "Whatever you build is a perfect duck. There is no right or wrong duck build."
5. Have everyone who built a duck stand back-to-back with someone who has yet to build a duck.
6. The one who built a duck instructs their partner on how to build the exact same duck. No peeking!
7. When they are finished, invite them to compare the ducks to evaluate their build.

Debrief

Ask the room to answer these questions:

1. What happened?
2. How did you work together to understand what you needed to build?
3. Did you learn anything new about the other person?
4. What does that tell us?
5. Now what might you do differently?

ACTIVITY NAME: HOW THE DUCK ARE YOU?

Why Use

To encourage sharing ideas, emotions, values, or simply validating other people's feelings through storytelling and expression.

When to Use

You can use this anytime you want to increase someone's ability to be open and to invite others to validate emotions and feelings. This is also a great activity to use with those who struggle with connecting or identifying their emotions or labeling emotions and sharing with others.

Resources

The LEGO® duck bricks to make a duck (for each person)

Time

Approximately 10 – 15 minutes:

1 minute to give the instructions
1 minute to build a duck
1 minute to modify the duck
2 – 5 minutes for sharing
3 minutes for debrief and reflection

Group Size

1+

Instructions

1. Give the builder(s) the six LEGO® duck bricks
2. Tell them they have one minute to build a duck.
3. When the ducks are complete, or in one minute, stop the building and comment on how the ducks are perfect.
4. Ask them to give the duck an emotion like happy, sad, or excited, by adding some additional bricks to the duck or around the duck.
5. Optional: You can also use cards with prompts if you want to encourage people to use new words or explore more challenging emotions.

   See the Strategic Play set of Emotion Cards with Negative and Positive words.
6. Once the builder has a duck and a duck emotion, ask a few prompt questions to help them connect the emotion and their duck in a story.
   a. How does the duck feel?
   b. How does the duck act when he feels this way?
   c. What does the duck say to his friends?
   d. What does the duck really want people to know?

Remember: If the builder says they built a duck, we all consider it to be a duck. There is no right or wrong duck or duck builder.

Debrief

- Congratulate everyone for making such great ducks and duck stories.
- Ask for volunteers who would like to share their story with the group.
- Invite listeners to acknowledge the duck's feelings simply by saying: Yes. I can see the duck feels [*add the storyteller's words*].

Online

This activity works great online. To do this well, ship people bags of multiple bricks and include the duck bricks inside the bag. Then have them find the duck bricks and run the above activity. Do not put a photo of the duck on the bag. If you do, they will just rebuild the photo.

ACTIVITY NAME:
DUCKING PARADISE

Why Use

To develop empathy and personal connections and to have fun.

Note: You can use this activity with any group by changing the instructions to make it more age-appropriate as needed.

When to Use

When you have more than an hour and you want an activity to build a team and create a positive and engaging environment.

Resources

Tables that seat 4 – 7 people
The LEGO® duck bricks to make a duck (for each person)
Colored pencils or crayons
Paper
Small bags of LEGO® bricks
You can add island themed music and snacks to set the mood for fun.

Time

Approximately 60 minutes:

Round One

2 minutes to give the instructions
2 minutes to build a duck

ACTIVITY NAME: DUCKING PARADISE | 23

2 minutes to name the duck
2 minutes to give the duck special skills
2 minutes to draw an island
2 minutes to name the island
5 minutes to build with LEGO bricks and label the builds
15 minutes to visit the other islands and build gifts
10 minutes to share stories
15 minutes to debrief

Group Size

5+

Instructions

1. Give the builder(s) the six LEGO® duck bricks
2. Explain they have one minute to build a duck.
3. When the ducks are complete, or in one minute, stop the building and comment on how the ducks are perfect.

4. Explain the duck is their new companion.
5. Ask them to name the duck and give it some special qualities.
6. Explain that they were together with their duck on a boat, but there was a bad storm and they were shipwrecked. They are lucky, however, because the duck was able to fly overhead and lead the way to this great island where they can now live.
7. Hand out the paper and colored pencils.
8. Ask everyone to draw an outline of their deserted island.
9. Ask them to name the island, being sure to include their name along with the duck's. They can name it something like: Jacquie's and Flappy's Hideaway.
10. They can now use colored pencils to draw a natural habitat, which may include trees, water, birds, etc. Remember, the duck brought you to this island for a reason; include that reason.
11. Explain that some things washed up on shore. Show them the random LEGO pieces.
12. They are now able to each build three things with the LEGO. These are three things they can have on their island to help them survive.
13. Next to their items They place their items on the paper and then write on the paper to label each item.

14. When everyone is done building and labeling, ask them to stand up and move over to the next seat.
15. Ask everyone to study the new island and see what already exists.
16. They want to leave behind a gift, so they can build one thing out of LEGO for the island's owner. Remind them to think about the island's owner and consider what that person would find valuable and appreciate. Remember: Ducks like gifts, too!
17. After building the gift, they can leave a note that says what the gift is and who left it, e.g. a radio from Bob.
18. They continue to move around the table until they have visited each island and left gifts for the owners.
19. Once completed, each person returns to their island to find their gifts.

Storytelling

1. Ask everyone to take turns telling the group about their island and their ducks, including:
    a. The name of their island
    b. What they naturally have on the island and where the duck likes to play
    c. The objects they built for themselves with the LEGO and why
    d. The gifts they received

Online

This activity can work online if people have the bricks. To do this online you can ask people to build and present after each stage. To visit different people's island, you might ask participants to take photos and post their comments in a mural board or other line collaboration board. You are only limited by your imagination.

ACTIVITY NAME:
GET THE DUCK OUT OF HERE

Why Use

This activity creates excitement, gives people an opportunity to explore their surroundings, and brings novelty into a session.

When to Use

This is a great activity to do when you have access to alternative locations. It can quickly change the mood of any group. Use it when you want people to discover a new location or rediscover an old one.

ACTIVITY NAME: GET THE DUCK OUT OF HERE | 27

Resources

The LEGO® duck bricks to make a duck (for each person)
Smartphones or standalone cameras

Time

Approximately 20 minutes:

1 minute to give the instructions
2 minutes to build a duck
1 minute per person to introduce their duck to others
20 minutes to find a location and return to the room
10 minutes for the final share

Group Size

1+

Instructions

1. Give the builder(s) the six LEGO® duck bricks
2. Tell them they have one minute to build a duck.
3. When the ducks are complete, or in one minute, stop the building and comment on how the ducks are perfect.

Remember: If the builder says they built a duck, we all consider the model to be a duck. There is no right or wrong duck or duck builder.

Step Two

Ask participants to pair and share—*see Duck, Networking* —and introduce their ducks to other ducks in the room. Continue until everyone has introduced their duck.

Step Three

Explain it is time to take the ducks out for a field trip and they need to bring along their smartphones or cameras.

Note: Some people may not have a camera. If this is the case, ask them to pair up with someone who does.

Explain that the duck has never left its pond and it is now ready to explore (add location: city, village, department, office, school, etc.).

Step Four

Each participant is now challenged to take their duck to a new and interesting location. Suggest they try to find a location the builder would also like to visit.

- If you are discovering a city or town, they might find a historic landscape, restaurant, or park.
- If you are discovering a new school, it could be the best place to study, get coffee, or meet a friend.
- If you are discovering a new office, it could be the photocopy room, lunchroom, or someone's desk.

Step Five

Take a photo of your duck.

Step Six

Participants return to the workshop room with their ducks and photos.

Step Seven

Pair and share again with the photos. Each person shows their photo and explains the location they selected. Ask them to expand on why they picked this location. Why was it interesting, attractive, or fun?

Debrief

- Congratulate everyone for making such great ducks and duck adventure stories.
- Ask for volunteers who would like to share their story with the group.
- Invite others to ask questions about the ducks and their adventures.

Online

You can also do this activity online by posting the photographs onto a mural or other collaborative board that people can share via Post-it Notes.

ACTIVITY NAME:
THE KARDUCKIANS

Why Use

This activity creates excitement and gives people an opportunity to explore new things or promote ideas, products, and services.

When to Use

Use this activity when you want to explore locations, services, or products. Use if you want people to become engaged supporters of something new or if you want to create exposure.

Resources

The LEGO® duck bricks to make a duck (for each person)
Smartphones with cameras or standalone cameras

Time

Approximately 20 minutes:

1 minute to give the instructions
2 minutes to build a duck
1 minute per person to introduce their duck to others
20 minutes to find a location and return to the room
10 minutes for the final share

Group Size

1+

ACTIVITY NAME: THE KARDUCKIANS | 31

Instructions

1. Give the builder(s) the six LEGO® duck bricks
2. Explain they have one minute to build a duck.
3. When the ducks are complete, or in one minute, stop the building and comment on how the ducks are perfect.

Remember: If the builder says they built a duck, we all will consider the model to be a duck. There is no right or wrong duck or duck builder.

Step Two

Ask participants to pair and share—see *Duck, Networking*—and introduce their ducks to other ducks in the room. Continue until everyone has had a chance to introduce their duck.

Step Three

Explain to everyone that their duck, the Karduckian, is a famous influencer with millions of followers. They are excited to promote a new product. It could also be a location, a service, a new course, a school, etc.

Note: Some people may not have a camera. If this is the case, ask them to pair up with someone who does.

Step Four

Each participant is now challenged to find creative ways their duck can interact with this new product, location, service, etc.

Step Five

Each participant needs to take a photo of their duck. Challenge them to consider what might make an interesting photo.

Step Six

Participants return to the workshop room with their ducks and photos.

Step Seven

Pair and share again with the photos.

This time the builder/photographer is acting like a researcher and speaks less.

Each person shows the photo to a partner. This time, the person viewing the duck photo plays the active role. They view the photo and tell the builder/photographer what they see. The builder listens and then documents the comments, similar to how one might caption a photo. Once the viewing person has had time to comment, the builder can share their ideas and/or build on the ideas. Now the partners reverse roles.

Step Eight

Repeat this process until everyone has shared or you run out of time.

Debrief

- Congratulate everyone for their ideas and posts.
- Ask for volunteers who would like to share their story with the group.
- Invite others to ask questions about the ducks/photos.

This activity works great online, too, with a small adjustment. You need to use a system that will allow you to create breakout groups.

This activity works great online . To do this well, ship people bags of multiple bricks and include the duck bricks inside the bag. Then have them find the duck bricks and run the above activity. Do not put a photo of the duck on the bag. If you do, they will just rebuild the photo. You can use any online board to share the photos back with the group.

ACTIVITY NAME: WHERE THE DUCK ARE YOU?

This is fun when you have a safe location for people to explore. This activity is like a treasure hunt, with the treasure being a duck.

Why Use

To create excitement and engagement and provide new challenges where groups or teams can work together. Optional: You can add a self-evaluation score for teams to consider their individual and group performance.

When to Use

Anytime you have a group that would benefit from teamwork, problem-solving and decision-making, and/or building deeper levels of engagement and connections.

Resources

The LEGO® duck bricks to make a duck (for each person)
Paper and pens to write clues

Time

75+ minutes:

1 minute to give the instructions
2 minutes to build a duck
2 minutes to modify the duck
5 minutes to explain the activity
50 minutes to run the activity
15 minutes to debrief
5 minutes to retrieve the ducks

Group Size

6+

Instructions

1. Give the builder(s) the six LEGO® duck bricks
2. Tell them they have one minute to build a duck.
3. When the duck is complete (or in one minute) stop the building and comment on how the duck is perfect.

Remember: If the builder says they built a duck, we all consider it to be a duck. There is no right or wrong duck or duck builder.

Step One

If you have enough people, create multiple teams. Tip: When problem-solving, the best teams have an odd number of people. Teams of three, five, or seven are perfect.

Step Two

The new teams combine their ducks to create a flock.

Step Three

Ask the teams to think of a location where they can put their flocks. You will provide guidelines for site selection, such as: You cannot leave the building, school, village, etc. And you may need to add rules such as: ducks can be no higher than 4 ft off the ground, they cannot be hidden from sight, etc. To ensure the teams have selected appropriate locations, you may want to them to get your approval before they leave. Stagger the times groups are leaving so they do not all leave together.

Step Four

When they have placed the flock in their chosen location, the teams return to the training room or classroom.

Step Five

Each team needs to write five good clues. The clues should be challenging but not impossible to understand. The easiest way to do this is for the teams to hide their flocks and then work backwards to create their clues for the other teams to follow.

Step Six

Send the teams out on their hunt, with a timeframe for when they must return.

Step Seven

(Optional: Use for Team Development and Reflection)

Add a scoring system that determines success, balancing the challenge with the ability to solve it. You want the teams to find the ducks by the end of the session, but not so quickly that there is no degree of difficulty. You can create your own point system that works for your learning outcomes. See below Point System examples:

3 points for finding your assigned flock
3 points for any flock located within the last 15 minutes (or another set time)
3 points for the most creative flock location
3 points for the most challenging clues
3 points for the team that most creatively deciphers the clues
3 points for the most engaging flock name
3 points for the team that has the most fun
3 points for the team that works best together

Step Eight

Once the activity is over, you can now add up the score. But there is a twist:

Individuals interview members of opposing teams and ask a series of reflective questions on a scale of 1-3 (one is low three is high):

1. Did you have fun?
2. Did your team work well together? 1 – 3
3. How would you rate your team performance? 1 – 3
4. How would you rate your individual performance? 1 – 3

Depending on time, interviewers can ask for examples to justify the score.

The interviewer hands the score sheet to the team member they "evaluated," so they can return to their team and finish their self-evaluation by adding in the additional scores above.

ACTIVITY NAME: SUPERHERO DUCK

Use this activity to support mental health, build self-awareness and self-esteem, and to support teams and team development. You can modify this activity by explaining that the duck has encountered a problem in its life. But the duck has been able to resolve the issue by accessing and utilizing a specific product, service, or new innovation you describe.

When to Use

When you want to create positive connections to self and others or to products and services.

Resources

The LEGO® duck bricks to make a duck (for each person)
Arts and crafts materials or additional LEGO® bricks

Time

Approximately 40 – 60 minutes. You can make this longer if you want to introduce the attributes of a product, service, or new innovation.

1 minute to give the instructions
2 minutes to build a duck
2 minutes to modify the duck

Group Size

1+

Instructions

Step One

1. Give the builder(s) the six LEGO® duck bricks
2. Explain they have one minute to build a duck.
3. When the ducks are complete, or in one minute, stop the building and comment on how the ducks are perfect.

Remember: If the builder says they built a duck, we all consider it to be a duck. There is no right or wrong duck or duck builder.

Step Two

1. Participants name their ducks.
2. Tell each builder their duck has been named a national hero.
3. Now ask them to make one modification to the Duck that would help tell a duck hero story. "What can you add to your duck to show it is a hero?"
4. Give the duck three hero attributes. They can be something a superhero might have, like the ability to see through walls; or the duck can have human hero qualities, like standing for truth.

5. Ask the builders to create a short story using these four steps from the hero's journey, according to Joseph Campbell:
   a. The ordinary life of the duck. Describe an ordinary day for the duck, before becoming a hero.
   b. The duck gets the call to action. Something happened and only this duck can help. What was it?
   c. Describe the challenge and how the duck overcomes the obstacles.
   d. The duck returns to its friends and family as a hero. Describe the homecoming. Explain how the duck's friends and family have changed in the way they see and treat the duck now that it is a hero.

Debrief

There are several ways to debrief this activity. Here are some suggestions.

Personal development

a. Ask the builders to review their duck story and think of a time in their life when they were a hero (use a life example). What similarities or differences are there when they compare and contrast with their own hero story? What are they most proud of?
b. Ask each builder to review their duck story and write a new story, only this time they are the duck. They are the hero. What could they overcome in their own life that could happen in the same way the duck overcame its challenges? What is their call to action?
c. Write a personal reflection on this activity and share it with a trusted friend, coworker, or teammate.

Product development

Ask the builders to review their duck story and consider the value the product brought forward during a challenging time. How could they strengthen their story to showcase the value of the product? Which elements of the story could they use or modify to communicate the product story to end users or potential end users?

Share with your team or department.

Service development

Ask each builder to review their duck story and consider the value the service offered during a challenging time. How could they strengthen their story to illustrate more value or hidden values? Which elements of the story could they use or modify to communicate the service story to end users or potential end users?

Share with your team or department.

New Innovation

Ask each builder to review their duck story and consider the value the new innovation brought forward during a challenging time. How could they strengthen their story to illustrate more value or hidden values? Which elements of the story could they use or modify to communicate the innovation story to end users or potential end users?

Share with your collaborators.

This activity works great online. To do this well, ship people bags of multiple bricks and include the duck bricks inside the bag. Then have them find the duck bricks and run the above activity. Do not put a photo of the duck on the bag. If you do, they will just rebuild the photo. You may choose to use breakout rooms for pairing and sharing.

ACTIVITY NAME: DUCKING DETAILS

Use this activity as a fun way for people to focus on the importance of observation and paying attention.

When to Use

This short activity is perfect for a classroom or boardroom where conversations are focused on visual identification.

Resources

The LEGO® duck bricks to make a duck (for each person)

Paper and pencils

Time

Approximately 20 minutes:

1 minute to give the instructions
2 minutes to build 2 ducks

Group Size

1+

Round One

1. The instructor builds the first two ducks before the program starts and hides them from view. The ducks have some small difference in how they are built.

For round one, the instructor might make the difference obvious to help the participants get the idea.

2. Explain that this activity is based on observation skills.
3. Ask the participants to look at the two objects and see if they can find how they are different. They can write each difference down on their note paper.
4. After the participants have finished writing down their observations, ask someone to go first to share one difference between the two ducks. Allow different participants to answer until the group has uncovered the differences.

Round Two

1. Ask the participants to find a partner and decide who will build and who will guess.
2. Give each team of two, two duck sets to build. As the one builds, the other looks away.

3. The builder must make two ducks with some differences.
4. The guesser is then able to turn around and look at the ducks to find what is different between the two.

Optional

If you want to add more fun, you can add a beat the clock timer. The builder can set a timer to see if the guesser can identify all the differences before the time is up.

Debrief

Ask the participants:
1. How they would rate their observation skills.
2. Why they would give themselves that score.
3. How hard was this activity and why?
4. If anyone thought they found all the differences but then discovered they did not?
5. Where keen observation skills are required in their job?
6. Where else in the world are keen observation skills necessary?
7. What jobs require keen observation skills? Examples may include detective work, science, health care, copywriting, accounting, etc.

ACTIVITY NAME:
DUCKING VALUES

Use this to explore the meaning of values for your school, community, or organization. This could lead into a great discussion on ethics.

When to Use

When you want to make this topic more fun and engaging, but you also want to explore how people feel about important topics.

Resources

The LEGO® duck bricks to make a duck (for each person)
Post-it Notes
Pens
Random LEGO® bricks, including small parts like flowers, hats, flags, etc.

Time

Approximately 45 minutes:

1 minute to give the instructions
2 minutes to build a duck
2 minutes to modify the duck
40 minutes for discussion and debrief

Group Size

1+

ACTIVITY NAME: DUCKING VALUES | 45

Instructions

1. Give the builder(s) the six LEGO® duck bricks
2. Explain they have one minute to build a duck.
3. When the ducks are complete, or in one minute, stop the building and comment on how the duck is perfect.

Remember: If the builder says they built a duck, we all consider it to be a duck. There is no right or wrong duck or duck builder.

Step One

1. Give an example of a human value, such as honesty or empathy.
2. Ask everyone to give their duck a human value by adding something to the build that would illustrate a value.
3. Create groups of two or three people who do not know each other very well. Ask each person to share their value and why they chose it.
4. Ask the participants to share their stories and include why this value is important to have in a particular situation, like at work, school, or in the community.

Debrief Options

- Ask everyone to share if they think the value is necessary and why.
- Ask the participants to think of a time where the value they selected could be compromised. For example, someone might state honesty. What if someone asks them if they like their new haircut, but they do not and want to avoid hurting the person's feelings with their honest opinion. Ask people to share if something like this has happened to them or someone they know.
- Now ask everyone what might happen if no one held this value.

You can go as deeply as you like with this activity, depending on the group. Imagine using this with ten-year olds in a classroom or in a boardroom discussion with health care workers dealing with ethics.

ACTIVITY NAME: I NEED A DUCKING HOLIDAY

Use this activity to engage a group and have some fun while being separated.

When to Use

When people are travelling or going on vacation or are going to be apart. This is a fun way to close a conference because the duck can become a transitional object linking the event with home or a home-based office.

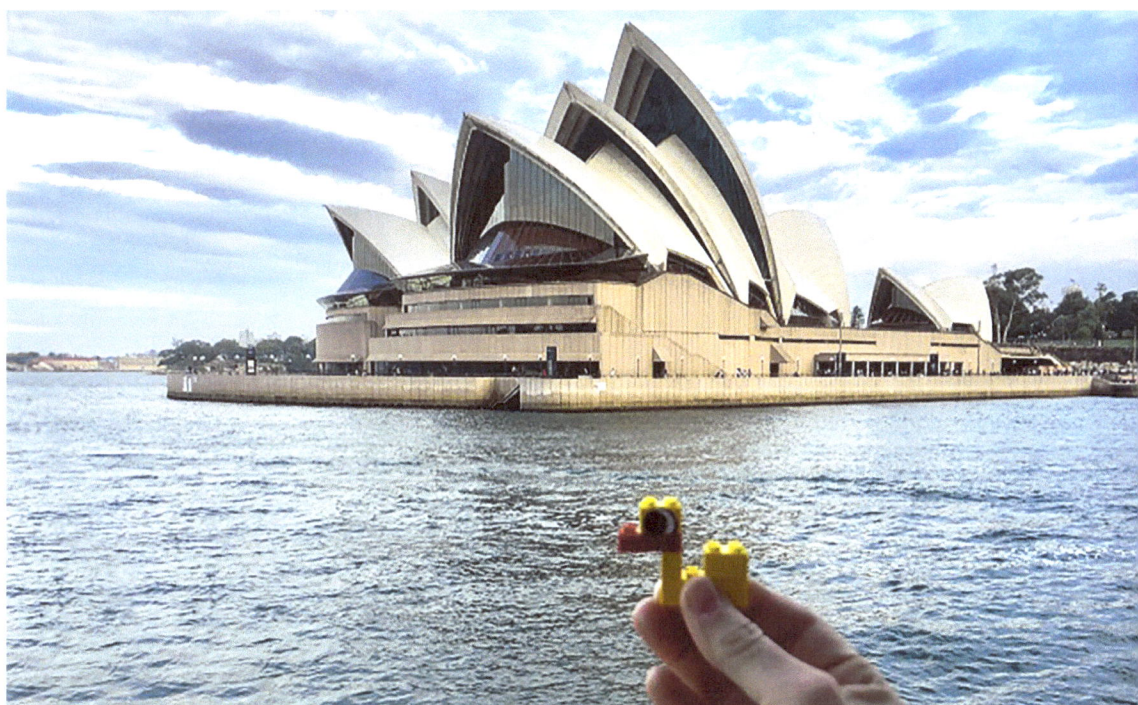

Resources

The LEGO® duck bricks to make a duck (for each person)
A camera
Some type of travel plans

Time

Approximately 10 minutes:

1 minute to give the instructions.
2 minutes to build a duck.
The time it takes to find a location, snap a photo and post in social media or a message board.

Group Size

1+

Instructions

1. Give the builder(s) the six LEGO® duck bricks
2. Explain they have one minute to build a duck.
3. When the ducks are complete, or in one minute, stop the building and comment on how the ducks are perfect.

Remember: If the builder says they built a duck, we all consider it to be a duck. There is no right or wrong duck or duck builder.

Instructions

1. Ask everyone to take their duck with them as they travel.
2. The challenge is to find interesting places to take photos of the duck. They might find spots at the airport or train station, while having lunch in a café, riding a bus, or buying fruit.
3. If people come from different countries, ask them to take a photo of their duck in front of something that will be fun and recognizable to others, like the Sydney Opera House, The Eifel Tower, the Golden Gate Bridge, or the Mountains in Whistler.
4. Develop a message board where people can post their photos and others can comment.

We have been running this activity for years. We started to take photos and post them and we saw that other people started to do this and send them to us. We can never get enough ducking photos. When posting online, feel free to use #strategicplayduck so we can all enjoy them!

ACTIVITY NAME: DUCK HUNTING

Why Use

This activity is a wonderful way to get people outside and exploring the world around them. It is fun and interactive, and it works well with teams/partners or for individuals.

When to Use

This is a great activity if you want people to quickly find something, like when exploring a college campus or finding new areas of a village or town.

Resources

The LEGO® duck bricks to make a duck (for each person)

Smartphones

Scavenger locations (you must identify these for your location)

Maps (optional)

Time

Approximately 60 minutes, or more, depending on the location:

1 minute to give the instructions
2 minutes to build a duck
2 minutes to modify the duck
5 minutes to group people into teams or pairs if this will not be an individual assignment

ACTIVITY NAME: DUCK HUNTING | 51

5 minutes to hand out the sheets and give people time
(insert the time for the hunt)
20 minutes or more to reconnect and look at the photos

Group Size

1+

Instructions

1. Give the builder(s) the six LEGO® duck bricks
2. Explain they have one minute to build a duck.
3. When the duck is complete, or in one minute, stop the building and comment on how the ducks are perfect.

Remember: If the builder says they built a duck, we all consider it to be a duck. There is no right or wrong duck or duck builder.

4. Split the group into pairs or teams.
5. Ask them to find all the locations on the Scavenger List.
6. As a team, they must go to the locations with their ducks and take photos of the ducks in front of the locations. The ducks are their proof they went to the location and did not just grab a photo from the Internet.
7. If you want everyone to stay together as a team, you can insist the team take a duck selfie in front of the location. If you want pairs to stay together, then one person takes the photo while the other places the duck in the location. They can get creative with this. If this is an individual activity, ask for a duck selfie.

Optional

8. If you want to add more fun, you can suggest they have one or two opportunities to call for help. If they use this option, they must call the organizer for a clue. But this will cost them either time or points, depending on how you want to score the activity.

9. Have everyone meet in a chosen location at a set time when you want them back. We usually do this in a restaurant and have snacks ready for when they arrive.
10. When all the teams have returned, you can review their team's photos to ensure they were at these locations.

Declare the Ducking Winner!

Note: We do this activity in the Ski Resort Town of Whistler, and one location is a bobsled. One team from the Austrian Marketing University could not find the correct location, so they sat on a bench and pretended they were riding a bobsled. Get ready for some serious fun, great photos, and occasional ingenious solutions when teams get stumped!

ACTIVITY NAME: FLOCKING THE DUCK

Why Use
This is a great team bonding activity.

When to Use
This activity works well to solidify new teams or to reengage existing teams.

ACTIVITY NAME: FLOCKING THE DUCK | 55

Resources

The LEGO® duck bricks to make a duck (for each person)

Time

Approximately 20 minutes:

1 minute to give the instructions
2 minutes to build a duck
2 minutes to modify the duck
15 minutes to share

Group Size

6+

Instructions

Step One

1. Give the builder(s) the six LEGO® duck bricks.
2. Tell them they have one minute to build a duck.

3. When the ducks are complete, or in one minute, stop the building and comment on how the ducks are perfect.

Remember: If the builder says they built a duck, we all consider it to be a duck. There is no right or wrong duck or duck builder.

Step Two

1. Ask participants to name their ducks and give them any human quality. For example: This is Sam. He has a big heart and is very emotional.
2. Ask the participants to pair off and share their ducks and stories.
3. Ask the pairs to now combine into teams of 4. This time, the pair partners introduce each other's ducks to the others: Let me introduce Sam. He wears his heart on his sleeve.
4. If you have a large group, you can make one more group of 8.
5. Once you have larger groups, either 4 or 8, you can now create a Duck FLOCK.
6. The group will need to name their flock based on something they feel binds or connects them. They will need to listen to each other and ask clarifying questions to discover the connection.
7. Ask the group to create a small landscape with their ducks. This about the shape and the composition of the ducks and where and how they should be placed.
8. Take a Flock Photo.

Options: You can ask them to create a tagline for the flock or even a cheer they can perform.

ACTIVITY NAME: ROCK THE DUCK

Why Use

This is a great team bonding activity.

When to Use

This activity works well to solidify new teams or to reengage existing teams.

Resources

The LEGO® duck bricks to make a duck (for each person)

Time

Approximately 60 minutes:

1 minute to give the instructions
2 minutes to build a duck
2 minutes to modify the duck
10 minutes to sort into teams and hear stories
30 minutes to work out the answers to the questions
15 minutes to share back to the larger group

Group Size

6+

This activity follows the same steps as the Duck Flock, but now the flock is a popular rock band.

Note: The teams could opt to be an orchestra or other type of ensemble, so do not feel obligated to limit the flocks to rock.

Instructions

1. Bring all the ducks together.
2. Each person names their duck and introduces them to the group.
3. Each builder identifies which instrument their duck might play.
4. The teams create a name for their new duck band.
5. Each teams now works to identify its duck band's greatest hit. What is the title of their number one record or song?
6. Every band needs an album cover, so create it by placing the ducks in a landscape that has a significant or value added background.
7. Make sure the ducks are showcased on the cover in a way that illustrates or connects to their musical personalities.
8. They can add anything else they like to create a short band story.
9. Select one storyteller to share.
10. The groups shares their stories back to the larger group via the storyteller.
11. Make sure you take a photo of your band's album cover.

ACTIVITY NAME: PRODUCKTIVITY

Imagined by our Curriculum Designer: Maxine King

Why Use

To help people reflect on what they need to be most productive and do their best work.

When to Use

When you want to have a good time and a few laughs, change the pace or tone of the room, or have people reflect on what they need to be productive. This activity works great for anyone who works on a project, online, or who depends on others to get their work done.

Resources

The LEGO® duck bricks to make a duck (one kit per group)
Blindfolds (optional)
Timer (optional)

Time

Approximately 30+ minutes:

3 minutes to join a group of six
2 minutes to determine one volunteer who will receive instructions and build
5 minutes to give the directions
10 minutes for the team members to take turns adding to the duck build
10 minutes for the groups to jointly reflect on the process
10 minutes for the large group to process the value of the exercise and its constraints: lack of visual cues, limited time, unclear instructions

Group Size

6 +

Instructions

- Ask people to form group(s) of six and create a circle
- Ask everyone to close their eyes
- Ask for a volunteer from each group to build
- Ask everyone else in the group to close their eyes
- No talking allowed

Round One

- Participants keep their eyes shut as they pass the duck around to each person in the group. They can have about 30 seconds each to feel the duck in their hands and then pass it to the person next to them.
- Everyone examines the finished product, keeping in mind that it does not matter how it is constructed. It is the result of the communication system used during the build
- After the duck has gone around the circle, return the duck to the builder.

Round Two

- Now that everyone has blindly examined the duck, the group will attempt to rebuild it.
- As everyone remains silent, give the volunteer builder a set of duck bricks; they will distribute a brick to each person in the group except for the person who will start; they will get two bricks.
- After builder one snaps the bricks together for memory, they will pass it to the next person who will add their brick.
- Continue passing the duck around the circle until each person has added their brick where they think it belongs.

Round Three

- The big reveal: Is the finished product correct?
- If yes, how did they do it?
- If no, why not? What happened?
- Ask the group to reflect on what happened in the process and how they may have supported and/or detracted from the build.
- You might witness and comment or question the following:
- Did anyone take someone else's work apart thinking they were helping?
- Did anyone want to take the duck apart and rebuild it? Why or why not?
- Did anyone sneak a peek? If so, did it help at all?
- Did anyone just give up or get frustrated?
- Did anyone blame anyone else?
- Did anyone just laugh or refuse to try?

Round Four

- Small group discussion on the process: impact of this *waterfall* activity, the roles people played, what might help if they were to do this again.
- Have them compare and contrast this activity to the way they work now.
- Do things ever go wrong but no one checks?
- Is it safe to check or ask for help if you are unsure?
- Do people ever take apart the work of others?
- What do you do if someone does not take the work seriously?

Add any debrief questions you want to reflect on what happened in the activity.

ACTIVITY NAME: GET YOUR DUCKS IN A ROW

Why Use

To have fun and help people think quickly on their feet.

When to Use

You can use this anytime you want to have fun with a group or change the mood. It is a great activity for teaching acceptance and "yes and" thinking.

Resources

The LEGO® duck bricks to make a duck (for each person)

Time

Approximately 20+ minutes:

1 minute to give the instructions
2 minutes to build a duck
2 minutes to explain the rules
15+ minutes to create a story

Group Size

6+

Note: You can do this with four people, but you will need to change the story framework to four steps.

Instructions

- Ask everyone to build a small duck.
- When the time is up, ask the participants to hold up their ducks.

Round One

- Ask everyone to think about what their duck is doing. Many people will say something like swimming, diving, thinking, flying, resting, etc.

Round Two

- Remind them of a simple story everyone knows, maybe Goldilocks and the Three Bears, Hansel and Gretel, Snow White, or Little Red Riding Hood. Using the hero's journey, quickly map out the story from the main character's perspective.

1. Ordinary life: Heading through the woods to Grandma's house.
2. Call to action: She meets up with the wolf and become suspicious
3. Answer the call: She uses clever thinking to outwit the wolf.
4. The battle: The wolf tries to eat Little Red Riding Hood; she screams and runs.
5. The prize: The woodsman comes with an axe, kills the wolf, and they find Grandma.
6. Back to ordinary life: Little Red Riding Hood has a new friend.

Round Three

- Now the new story is about the duck. The storytellers form a line across the room.
- Ask for one volunteer who can use their duck to start the story with: *Once upon a time there was a duck (living an ordinary life, which they explain).*
- The next person goes to the end of the line with their duck and adds the last part of the story. This includes how the duck has been transformed as it returns to its ordinary life. And the storyteller finishes by declaring, "The end."
  Note: *This forms the story's frame.*
- Ask for someone to share what happens in the middle. They will take their duck and go to the middle, explaining either the call to action, the battle, or the prize.
- Ask for two more volunteers to do the last two steps.

Round Four

Now start from the beginning again. This time, allow everyone to add to the story to give it a bit more color or detail.

Round Five

(optional) Ask the group if they would like to try it again, this time weaving in a theme like the name of their school, town, company, service, or product. You can even use this method to tell the story of a company legacy or vision or to map out a conflict situation in a fun way.

Debrief

Ask people to comment on their experience of creating a story so quickly; remember to congratulate them on their efforts. You can connect this to the process of brainstorming and allowing ideas to build from each other. The more you exercise this creative practice, the better you will be at building on each other's ideas.

This activity works great online. To do this well, ship people bags of multiple bricks and include the duck bricks inside the bag. Then have them find the duck bricks and run the above activity. Do not put a photo of the duck on the bag. If you do, they will just rebuild the photo.

ACTIVITY NAME: MANGEMENT, DUCK SUCCESS

As published in our previous book, Strategic Play: The Creative Facilitator's Guide#2: What the Duck

Why Use

To facilitate an opportunity to consider better ways to manage or work with product owners or project owners.

When to Use

Anytime you want to create some fun and opportunities for leadership reflection.

Resources

The LEGO® duck bricks to make two small ducks

Time

Do the math based on the numbers in your group:

3 minutes to give the instructions
1 minute for the manager to build the first duck
30 seconds for each person to give instructions to the next player
1 minute for the last builder to build the final duck product
5 – 10 minutes to discuss the process or method used and compare and contrast to the work environment.

Group Size

3+

You can add more players if you think it is valuable. Be creative and give them roles based on the environment where you are working, such as consultant, project manager, team leader, supervisor, CEO, or board member.

Instructions

Note: *This game is played in a similar way to the childhood game of "telephone."*

- One person is assigned the manager role.
- One person is assigned the builder role.
- All other players are middle managers and only pass on information about the building of the duck.
- Everyone stands in a long line. The manager is at one end of a line and the builder is at the other end of the line.
- **Step one:** The manager builds a duck without anyone seeing the duck.
- **Step two:** The manager tells the first person in line how to make the duck and quickly shows person one the duck they want the builder to make.
- **Step three:** The first "middle manager" tells the next "middle manager" how to build the duck, without letting them see the model.
- **Step four:** The middle managers continue down the line, relaying the information, until the last middle manager describes the process to the builder.

Debrief

Compare the first duck to the final duck, and see if the result is anywhere close to what the manager wanted.

Ask the participants:

1. What happened?
2. What went right? What went wrong?
3. What can we learn about this and how is it the same or different from the way we are working right now?

Success

We ran this activity with members of the USAF at the Squadron Officer School, only to find out that one team succeeded perfectly. We had never seen this before. They had developed a very effective way to exchange information in the field, and they applied those learnings to this activity. Unfortunately, due to state secrets, we cannot disclose their hidden advantage. But we can confirm it is possible to get the correct outcome, so have fun trying to figure out this puzzle with your team or group. Now that's a ducking challenge!

ACTIVITY NAME:
SNADU (SITUATION NORMAL ALL DUCKED UP)

Why Use

The ability to work as part of a team is a workplace expectation; however, individuals may not realize the role they play. This activity can provide insight and a fun way to engage a team.

When to Use

You can use this activity when a team is newly created or when an existing team needs insight into how they function.

Resources

The LEGO® duck bricks to make a duck (one kit per group)
Blindfolds (optional)
Smartphones (timer) and cameras (optional)

Time

Approximately 30+ minutes:

3 minutes to join a group of six
2 minutes to determine one volunteer who will receive instructions and build
5 minutes to give the directions to build the duck and for the volunteer to build it
10 minutes to reflect on the process in the small group
10 minutes for the large group to process the value of the exercise and its constraints: lack of visual cues, limited time, and unclear instructions

ACTIVITY NAME: SNADU (SITUATION NORMAL ALL DUCKED UP)

Group Size

6 +

Instructions

- Ask people to form groups of six.
- Ask for a volunteer to build (this person will close their eyes or be blindfolded)
- Give the volunteer the duck bricks.
- Set the timer to 1 minute for each instruction.
- Taking turns, each participant will have 1 minute to provide a verbal instruction to the volunteer who will add one brick to build a small duck.
- Each participant will need to pay attention to the role they played in this process.

Round One

Examine the finished product, keeping in mind that it does not matter how it is constructed; it is the result of the communication system used during the build.

Round Two

Each participant should report how they believe they contributed to the build.

Round Three

Small group debrief or a self-reflection for each person and how they contributed to the build, how the volunteer experienced receiving instructions, and how they were able to process the information they received to build.

Round Four

Large group discussion on the process: impact of verbal instruction with no visual cues, the roles people played, the importance of clear instruction. Did people follow the rules?

ACTIVITY NAME: BEYOND THE DUCK POND

As published in our previous book, Strategic Play: The Creative Facilitator's Guide#2: What the Duck

Why Use

To conduct a check-in or a debrief, or to get feedback.

When to Use

Anytime you want to know how people are doing or how they are feeling within a process.

Resources

The LEGO® duck bricks to make a duck (for each person)

Set of instructions for building

Time

5 minutes:

1 minute to give the instructions
1 minutes to build a duck
1 minute to place your duck in the pond

Group Size

2+

Instructions

1. Give the builder(s) the six LEGO® duck bricks and have them build any duck in one minute.
2. Draw a big duck pond on flip chart paper with different areas (fresh water for relaxing and resting, fun area for splashing and playing, deep water indicating "over my head," shallow area indicating too easy and not challenging enough, stagnant or polluted water for trouble, and so on.
3. Put the paper on a table or flat surface.
4. Have the participants place their ducks indicating how they think they are doing at any given time in the session (they can write their names by their duck) or in a debrief at the end of the session. Ask them to make at least one recommendation to improve the session.

   This is an instant feedback loop regarding how your session is flowing! You can choose to make adjustments or have a conversation, only you know what fits and makes sense once you see your duck pond scattergram.

Option Two: Use the Flow Chart and have the ducks placed on the chart to see where people are in the state of flow or the zone.

Option Three: If you know anything about polarity management or Theory U, use the polarity management diagram and have people place their ducks in the polarity loop.

ACTIVITY NAME: BEYOND THE DUCK POND | 73

Option Four: Follow these simple steps to draw your own duck pond.

Start with the outline of your pond. We recommend including an inlet and an outlet: a stream at one end and a waterfall at the other.

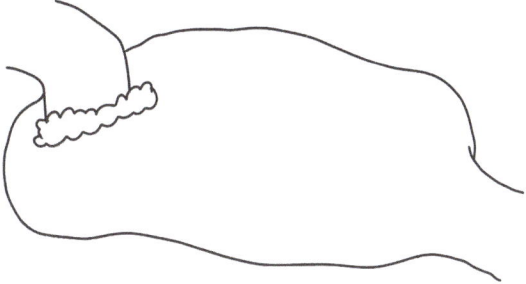

Decide where to put your different feeling areas of the pond. Try intermingling them out so the negative and positive areas are combined rather than clumped together. If you plan to place the pond with ducks on a table, keep in mind that people will be gathered around and viewing it from all sides. Be sure the text is aligned with its nearest side for easy reading.

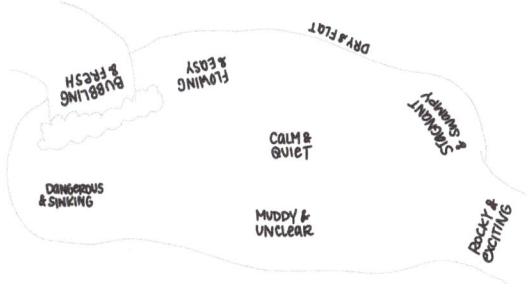

Add some characteristic details to enhance the different areas of the pond. You can include lines to show water movement, cloudiness, rocks, bubbles, and splashing water.

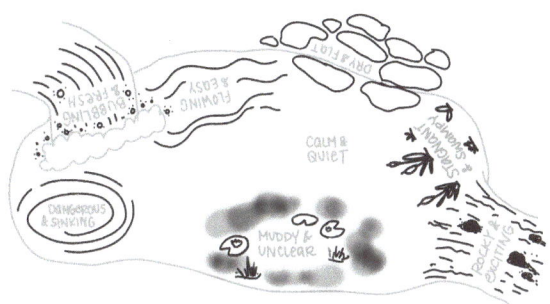

Embellish as little or as much as you want with other natural pond elements. Have fun with it!

A detailed digital color version, illustrated by Sarah Moyle, is also available for purchase on the Strategic Play website.

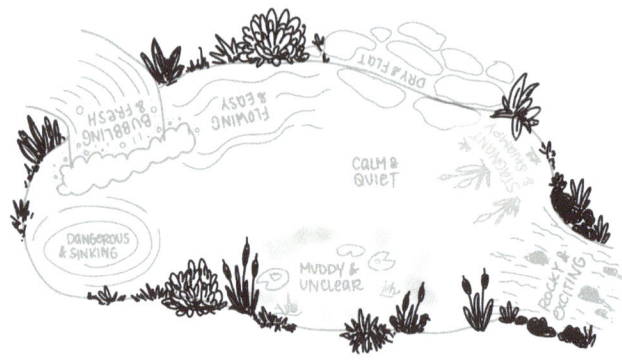

JOY & HAPPINESS WITH BRICKS

Over the years, on so many occasions, we have observed how LEGO just makes people happy. We decided to start documenting some of these observations on our blog. Here, we would like to share some of these posts with you to help broaden your appreciation for the bricks, too. And what better way to round out this book of LEGO activities than to acknowledge and dwell on our fondness for this amazingly diverse tool.

▬ LEGO® DUCK CONNECTION ▬

Have you ever found yourself sitting on an airplane or in a doctor's office, a bus stop, or even in traffic? Most of us will use this time to entertain ourselves by picking up our phones. Next time you are in this situation, just look around to see how many people are staring as they endlessly scroll.

What if you put your hand in your pocket and found 6 LEGO Bricks?

Next time you find yourself waiting, instead of reaching for your phone, simply pick up some bricks. Just looking at the bricks will make you feel happier, but imagine the look on strangers' faces as they glance over at you, and see you have LEGO and you are building a duck. Just watching you build with the bricks will make them feel happier too. This is known as mirror neurons, and it happens when people see people doing something they would like to do.

Now, if you really want people to pay attention. Build a duck and put it somewhere interesting. We took duck bricks to the top of Whistler Mountain and took our very good camera equipment with us. People could not help but stand around and watch us take photos of the duck. It is true, they stopped taking selfies and

started to stare. One person even came up to us and asked if they could take a photo of our duck.

We have all heard about these awful flights where the plane either doesn't take off or people are delayed on the flight. If you should find yourself in this situation, pull down the table and build a duck. To make this even more interesting, don't take a photo. Instead, take out your notebook. Study the duck and then make some notes. You can even sketch the duck. Watch and see what happens next. It's almost guaranteed someone will ask you what you are doing and ask why you have the duck.

They might tell you all about their grandchildren and what they are building. They might tell you they have so much LEGO at home etc.

If you don't like people, do not do this because you are guaranteed to make new friends. Needless to say, this is a great time to have your business card ready to hand out and do some networking.

POWER OF COLOR

We'd like to provide you with some other ideas on ways to use LEGO® to relax, find balance, and be happier.

We cannot walk past a LEGO store without going in and, of course, spending money. Why? Because we love LEGO. At least that's the answer we'd give if you asked us.

But have you ever wondered why you feel happy as soon as you see LEGO bricks? They tend to have this instant effect on people, making them smile. Maybe it's because as soon as they see the bricks, they remember the fun they had playing as a child, or maybe even when they were creating something just last week. Perhaps it's simply because the colors of the bricks make us feel good, playful, creative, open, and ready to explore.

As an art student and then an art therapist, Jacquie studied color and the use of color for many years. Although we might think the colors we pick are simply preference, there are reasons we might not be fully aware of regarding why we select the colors we do. In fact, there is a lot more behind color psychology than we might first consider.

While color is all around us in nature, trees, sky, flowers, and trees, it has only been in recent history that man has been able to manipulate the use of color by creating it. Only within the last 150 years or so have we had access to manufactured color, which we created with the synthesis of aniline dyes or coal-tar derivatives and metallic oxides.

Our interaction with color in the natural world has given us the ability to assign meaning to colors. That in turn helps us to make connections with the world around us. We might assign color and meaning to things, such as: green is healthy; yellow is happy; blue is calm; red means danger; pink means soft; orange means energy; purple means expensive, etc. Everyone has their own color code they use, and most of us have a favorite color.

As soon as we interact with colorful LEGO bricks, we are activating both our conscious and our subconscious mind. Research indicates color can be used to helps us to focus on details or to think bigger and activate our imagination. It can even be used to evoke memories. Color activates our minds. For many years, marketing companies have been using color to help drive consumer behaviors.

We have been lucky enough to tour the LEGO factory where they make these beautifully colored bricks and the factory where they package them. Even if you are not into production or manufacturing, it's hard not to be totally impressed with the amazing explosion of color. They do not allow photographs because their processing systems are their intellectual property. They did, however, give me a fun keepsake brick to prove we had been there.

The colors LEGO uses to create their bricks are carefully selected and limited to their in-house color guide. This uniformity of color is what attracts us to the bricks and makes our creations look so pleasing when we build. Imagine if every red brick was a different shade of red? Or if they used different colors on each brick? What if they used different colors for every brick or created a random variety of parts and pieces that you would never be able to find in your collection because they were never the same color? The very thought of this makes me cringe.

Next time you break open your bricks, spend some time and think about the colors and what each color means to you. Consider which colors you are attracted or connected to or which combination of colors you find most pleasing. Are there any colors you really don't like? Or are there ones you love and consider your favorite? Are there any colors you look for more often because they just make you feel happy? True confession: Jacquie loves the LEGO brick in what she calls Kelly Green—they make her smile!

What's your favorite color LEGO brick?

Time to Relax

1. Take a pile of LEGO bricks and divide them into colors only.
2. Now with each color group build one small model.
3. Take a look at the model you built and give it a name.
4. Create a story that explains what this model does. Use your imagination.
5. Repeat until you have all the bricks built into small models.
6. See if you can find a way to connect each small model into a big super story.

— DECONSTRUCTING

We'd like to provide you with some ideas on ways to use LEGO® to relax, find balance, and be happier.

When we run live events, it is common for clients to ask afterward if they can help us clean up the LEGO. We usually say something like "No, that's ok. You go home. We have a very specific way of sorting the LEGO for travel."

Now there is some honest truth to this, because we do have a system of taking photos of the models, removing the information from flip charts, and deconstructing and repacking the bricks. However, it would only take us a few minutes to show people so they could help pack us up the LEGO.

In reality, we like to put the LEGO bricks away ourselves because there is a therapeutic quality to this quiet activity.

As we take the models apart, we silently reflect on the participants' stories and the information they shared. As we remove each Minifigure, disconnect each connector, unsnap all the bricks, and pile everything into categories (not colors), we consider all the information the participants uncovered during the session.

It is nearly impossible to list all the things that go through our minds as we deconstruct the individual and shared models. However, as reflective practitioners, we ask ourselves things like:

- What happened?
- What went well?
- What could we have improved?
- Who do we need to follow up with?
- What might we include in our client debrief?
- How, when, and where did we notice the aha moments?
- What were the unspoken or unsaid moments people might be reflecting on now, either consciously or unconsciously?
- How do we feel as facilitators?
- What information do we need to share with each other as co-facilitators?
- What questions do we have for each other or for the organizer?
- Going forward, what might we do differently?

Many of these questions are happening in a dream-like flow zone, where the unconscious mind helps the conscious mind make sense of huge quantities of information.

As we take the time to clean up the room, and we always leave the room as we found it, we feel like a rock band leaving a show. We planned, we arrived, we presented, we packed up, and now we are off. It's a story with a beginning and an end. And if we unpack it, we see the hero's journey because there is always some kind of conflict and turning point. We load up the car with our well-organized materials ready to travel and with a great sense of accomplishment that can only come from a great session of SERIOUS PLAY!

The act of deconstructing the bricks after a workshop is relevant and important. Although we have been on our feet for hours, we happily tidy up. This process not only brings the story to a satisfying end but it sets the tone for the next session and helps us process valuable information.

The next time you are deconstructing your session's LEGO models, make sure you give yourself the gift of this valuable time to reflect in silence and congratulate yourself on a job well done.

And of course, one last reminder: Don't forget to wash your hands!

— THE SOUND OF BRICKS

We'd like to provide you with some ideas on ways to use LEGO® to relax, find balance, and be happier.

Let's forget about the amazing fun pieces for now, the colors, and the Minifigures. Let's just concentrate on the way the bricks connect. Lego bricks simply click together like nothing else. There is a very interesting reason why clicking together LEGO is so very satisfying.

Did you know all LEGO bricks click together and disconnect with the exact same amount of effort or velocity? You might think this has to do with the patent knob and tube construction. In part, this is correct. However, the real secret is in the plastic compound. How do I know this? Because when I was a Licensed Strategic Partner with the LEGO Group, I stumbled upon this very interesting factoid. The LEGO Systems Group put an enormous amount of effort into the chemicals and compounds that make up the plastic they use to make LEGO. They are very strict on this point because they understand the way the bricks click together and unclick—sometimes called clutch—is one of the important features of the bricks that makes them so irresistible.

This is just one reason it has taken LEGO such a long time to change the formula for the plastic to something more sustainable.

You might question this point if you have ever had trouble separating two bricks. The most frustrating of these moments for me is when two plates become stuck together, one on top of the other, requiring the LEGO tool to disconnect

them—the corner of another brick will also do the trick. From a physics standpoint, the plastic is not to blame: It is the design of the build that creates this strong bond. If you cannot get them to come apart, don't worry. Maybe the bricks are meant to be together. Maybe you are meant to let go and accept that things change.

Back to the sounds. Next time you want to relax and reflect, take two bricks and close your eyes. Click them together and then click them apart. Pay attention and listen to the sound they make while reflecting on the amount of energy used to put them together and take them apart. No matter how many times you repeat this process of connecting and disconnecting the bricks, they will make the same sound and take the same amount of energy.

In such a chaotic world, isn't it nice to know your bricks remain consistent?

This is just one of the things that makes playing with LEGO bricks so satisfying. It's the Joy of the Click.

If you have your own story of brick happiness, send it along. We would love to hear from you.

ORGANIZING BRICKS

We'd like to provide you with some ideas on ways to use LEGO® to relax, find balance, and be happier.

If you are a LEGO SERIOUS PLAY methods facilitator, there's a good chance you have lots of LEGO. If you are just starting out, you are probably planning all the ways you will build your collection. Having a large collection of LEGO is important, as is storing and organizing it so you can find the LEGO you need and be ready to facilitate events both large and small. At Strategic Play, we have gone through many variations of storing and sorting the bricks.

In the early years, LEGO insisted we purchase new bricks for each client that we worked with in a workshop. Working under contract, we were compelled to leave the bricks with the client so they could use the LEGO to continue conversations after the workshop. On the one hand, this was great. After a session, we would just leave the bricks on the table and walk out the door with a few Post-it Notes.

We quickly realized this theory the team would continue to build and discuss was unlikely to happen. After running a strategy session for a senior management team at a regional hospital, one of the doctors called and asked if I was coming back to pick up the LEGO? They had nowhere to store it and they were too busy to use it. Without me there to facilitate the conversations, people did not feel they had the ability to manage the time effectively. At the end of the day, this team donated the bricks to the pediatrics department. I could not help thinking that while this was great for the kids, it was a missed opportunity.

Then came the open source model and, with it, the idea to reuse the bricks. Yay! This opened up a whole new world. For clients, the cost of the workshops became much more reasonable. However, with this gift came the challenge: How do we manage the bricks after using them?

Phase One

We started by organizing the bricks back into their original sets: Starter kits, exploration kits, landscape kits, and connector kits. This was exhausting. Not only was it hard work, but it was impossible to maintain a perfect set. We realized this was way too much work, and as Stephen so eloquently put it, "The squeeze ain't worth the juice."

Phase Two

We then began to create our own kits, comprised of loose bricks that would amount to one small container with one Minifigure each. This small container was in fact about the size of a Starter Kit, but the bricks in each kit would be different. We created many of these using a large collection of pieces from Starter Kits. But more often, we would also mix in pieces from the Landscape Kits. Then we saw people were busy looking at each other's kits and complaining they were not the same. The element of fairness came into play; and yes, it created issues.

Phase Three

We now begin all sessions with a brand new Exploration Bag. We let people open the bags themselves and then we collect the packaging. We use the small collection of bricks to facilitate the skill building part of the session. After the first 30 – 45 minutes, we hand out small Ziploc bags and let people put these bricks away. We usually give these bricks to the participants as a transitional object, meaning they take the bricks back to the office to build on their desk. This is a great way for them to remember the session. The joy they feel receiving this small gift is well worth the cost. Then we move on to using larger containers of pre-enjoyed LEGO.

We start with new bricks where all the bricks are the same, and then transition to larger mixed-up kits. These large kits are large boxes, and we bring one for each table. They are mostly mixed-up pieces from Starter Kits. We remind people to use hand sterilizer before and after building. If anyone asks if they can use the bricks from another table, we encourage them to politely ask the other team or table group if they have a certain brick they are willing to trade. No stealing is allowed as we play well together.

This process makes setting up and cleaning up simple, easy, and stressless. The participants are happy because they each got a new bag of bricks to open and everyone had the same bricks. Not only does this meet their needs for fairness, but they receive an unexpected gift to keep. But also, and this is so very important, you are happy because you don't have the overwhelming job of hours of sorting LEGO bricks!

THE CURIOUS LITTLE LEGO DUCK

This last weekend we travelled to a more remote location in Mexico for my eldest son's wedding. My son met a wonderful young woman who is the fourth generation to live and play on a ranch about three hours from Mexico City. This made a perfect backdrop for this amazing wedding. Coming from Canada, we loved learning more about the people of this historic region, the culture, and of course we loved the sunny climate.

While we were getting our family photographs taken in the courtyard that dates back to 1710, I asked my husband to put my cell phone into his pocket for safe keeping. As he reached in, he discovered, What the Duck? He had a small stowaway in his inside suit jacket pocket. Yes, the curious little LEGO duck had come along for the ride.

As we dug out the pieces for the duck, we all laughed with delight when we saw it! My husband has no idea when he wore this suit last or why the duck would be in his pocket. We then included the duck in some of our family photos as a welcome reminder of how well the duck can travel and can hide in a pocket and create a welcome and unexpected surprise.

Have you ever reached into your pocket and found some LEGO that you might have put there and subsequently forgotten? The wedding was a very happy and joyful occasion, but it makes us wonder at how just a few small bricks tucked into your pocket can make you smile when you find them by a happy accident or on purpose.

We then took the duck with us to tour the Museum of Anthropology in Mexico City. After all, he had come a long way and deserved to have some fun while learning about this historic culture.

Do you have a LEGO duck story to share? If yes, please share it with us. We love to hear about your What the Duck moments!

CONCLUSION

As we continue our quest to grow the acceptance of play at all stages of life, we are amazed to see the people and organizations getting on board with us. It was a real game changer when we got to work with the U.S. Air Force and then they kept coming back. We saw this as undeniable proof there are no limits to where you can take the bricks and play to create positive change and solve problems of the utmost complexity. There will always be difficult challenges in our way. But by embracing the inherent optimism of play, we can learn to deal with these challenges to devise a path forward. And by spreading this optimism, we enable others to do the same.

REFERENCES

Ayres, R. U. (1994). Information, entropy, and progress: a new evolutionary paradigm. New York: American Institute of Physics (AIP),| c1994, 1.

Ayres, R. (2016). A Brief History of Ideas: Energy, Entropy and Evolution. InEnergy, Complexity and Wealth Maximization (pp. 15-54). Springer International Publishing.

Blatner, Adam (1996). Acting-In: Practical Applications of Psychodramatic Methods, Revised, 3rd Ed.

Brown, S. (2010). *Play: How it Shapes the Brain, Opens the Imagination and Invigorates the Soul.* Avery: New York.

Burgi, P., & Roos, J. (2003). Images of strategy. *European Management Journal, 21*(1), 69. Busch, P., Venkitachalam, K., & Richards, D. (2008). Generational differences in soft knowledge situations: Status, need for recognition, workplace commitment and idealism. *Knowledge & Process Management, 15*(1), 45-58.

Campbell, W. (2002). Consideration of consulting psychology/organizational educational principles as they relate to the practice of industrial-organizational psychology and the society for industrial and organizational psychology's education and training guidelines. *Consulting Psychology Journal: Practice and Research, 54*(4), 261-274.

Cascio, W., & Aguinis, H. (2008). Research in industrial and organizational psychology from 1963 to 2007: Changes, choices, and trends. *Journal of Applied Psychology, 93*(5), 1062-1081.

Csikszentmihalyi, M. (1987). *Finding Flow: The Psychology of Engagement With Everyday Life.* Basic Books.

Cohen, S., & Bailey, D. (1997). What makes teams work: Group effectiveness research from the shop floor to the executive suite. *Journal of Management, 23*(3). 239-290.

Edwards, B., Day, E., Arthur, W., & Bell, S. (2006). Relationships among team ability composition, team mental models, and team performance. *Journal of Applied Psychology, 91*(3), 727-736

Fein, G. "Pretend play: Creativity and consciousness." In Gorlitz, D. and J. F. Wohlwill. Eds. Curiosity, Imagination and Play. Hillside, NJ: Lawrence Erlbaum. 1987. 282–304.

Franco, L. (2008). Facilitating collaboration with problem structuring methods: A case study of an inter- organisational construction partnership. *Group Decision and Negotiation, 17*(4), 267-286.

Gauntlett, D. 2007. *Creative Explorations.* Routledge.

Gundlach, M., Zivnuska, S., & Stoner, J. (2006). Understanding the relationship between individualism- collectivism and team performance through an integration of social identity theory and the social relations model. *Human Relations, 59*(12), 1603-1632.

Harel, I., Papert, S. (Eds.). 1985-1990. *Constructionism: Research Reports and Essays, 1985 – 1990 by the Epistemology and Learning Research Group.* The Media Laboratory: Massachusetts Institute of Technology.

Isaksen, S. (2007). The climate for transformation: Lessons for leaders. *Creativity and Innovation Management, 16*(1), 3-15.

Hülsheger, U., Anderson, N., & Salgado, J. (2009). Team-level predictors of innovation at work: A comprehensive meta-analysis spanning three decades of research. *Journal of Applied Psychology, 94*(5), 1128-1145.

Hyland, M. (1988). Motivational control theory: An integrative framework. *Journal of Personality and Social Psychology, 55*(4), 642-651.

Karp, T. (2005). Unpacking the mysteries of change: mental modeling. *Journal of Change Management, 5*(1), 87-96.

Kaufman, J., & Beghetto, R. (2009). Beyond big and little: The four c model of creativity. *Review of General Psychology, 13*(1), 1-12.

Landy, F. J., & Conte, J. M. (2007). *Work in the 21st century: An introduction to industrial and organizational psychology* (2nd ed.). Malden, MA: Blackwell Publishing.

La Doux, J. (2003) The Emotional Brain, Fear, and the Amygdala: Cellular and Molecular Neurobiology, Vol. 23, Nos. 4/5, October 2003

Lencioni, P. (2002). *The five dysfunctions of a team.* San Francisco, CA: Jossey-Bass.

Leonard, H., & Freedman, A. (2000). From scientific management through fun and games to high performing teams: A historical perspective on consulting to team-based organizations. *Consulting Psychology Journal: Practice and Research, 52*(1), 3-19.

Locke, E., & Latham, G. (2002). Building a practically useful theory of goal setting and task motivation: A 35-year odyssey. *American Psychologist, 57*(9), 705-717.

Lloyd Smith, J., Meyerson, D., Walling S. (2017). Strategic play: What the duck! Activities for engagement with the Duck Bricks. Wordzworth Publishing.

Pink, D. 2006. *A Whole New Mind: Why Right-Brainers Will Rule The Future.* Penguin Books Ltd. London.

Prichard, J.S., & Stanton, N.A. (1999). Testing Belbin's team role theory of effective groups. *The Journal of Management Development, 18*(8), 652-665.

Roos, J., Victor, B. (1999). Towards a new model of strategy-making as serious play. *European Management Journal,* 17(4), 348–355.

Roos, J., Victor, B., and Statler M. (2004). Playing Seriously with Strategy. *Long- Range Planning*, 37(6), 549-568.

Rock, D. (2007) Your Brain at Work: Strategies for Overcoming Distraction, Regaining Focus, and Working Smarter All Day Long Harper Business.

Rock, D. (2009), Managing with the Brain in Mind. Strategy and Business issue 56, Autumn

Rieber, L. (1996). Seriously considering play: Designing interactive learning environments based on the blending of microworlds, simulations, and games. *Educational Technology Research and Development,* 44(2), 43-58.

Salopek, J. (1999). Stop playing games. *Training & Development, 53* (2), 28. Senior, B. (1997). Team roles and team performance: Is there 'really' a link?. Journal of

Stringer, E., T. (1996). *Action research: A handbook for practitioners.* Thousand Oaks, California: Sage Publications.

Sullivan, F. R. (2011). Serious and playful inquiry: Epistemological aspects of collaborative creativity. *Journal of Educational Technology & Society, 14* (1), 55-n/a.

Tangdhanakanond, K., Pitiyanuwat, S., & Archwamety, T. (2006). A development of portfolio for learning assessment of students taught by full-scale constructionism approach at darunsikkhalai school. *Research in the Schools, 13*(2), 24-36.

Widmeyer, W. N., & Ducharme, K. (1997). Team building through team goal setting. *Journal of Applied Sport Psychology,* 9:1,97-113.

www.ingramcontent.com/pod-product-compliance
Lightning Source LLC
Chambersburg PA
CBHW051154220526
45473CB00003B/773